—— THE ——
FRAGRANT GARDEN

Penhaligon's
Scented Treasury
of Verse and
Prose

THE
FRAGRANT GARDEN

Edited by Sheila Pickles

LONDON MCMXCII

For Ian and Anthea

INTRODUCTION

Dear Reader,

In our dreams and musings we all like to be transported into other worlds. While many people read science fiction or detective stories when they relax, I have always enjoyed reading gardening books. Over the years, I have come to realize that all garden writers write with a passion for their subject – their sentiments come straight from their hearts. Whether I read them at home or in a distant land, I am immediately transported to my garden – the one place where I long to be.

Nothing gives a gardener greater pleasure than to take a friend around their garden, pointing out a plant which has come on especially well, introducing them to a new species or simply picking a bunch of flowers for them to take home. Many of the greatest gardeners have been women, and we are fortunate that they were able to write of their ideas in a way that was both practical and inspiring. Gertrude Jekyll designed many gardens for houses built by the great architect Edwin Lutyens. Her books have become gardening classics and her influence is still felt today. Vita Sackville-West is well known for the garden she created with her husband, Sir Harold Nicolson, at Sissinghurst Castle, where they combined formal garden design with informal planting. Her witty gardening column in *The Observer* had encouraging words for those with either small plots or spacious landscapes. For the garden is a great leveller – the sun shines and the rain comes down on prince and pauper alike. Indeed some of the most charming gardens I know have been created by those who never knew a Latin name, but whose green fingers worked their own magic.

For me inner satisfaction comes from my own practical achievements in my garden. Creating something myself – having the idea, forming a plan, making it work, and seeing the results – is what I most enjoy. When I see the results, I feel like one of the world's makers, and I enjoy that sense of satisfaction reflected in many of the extracts I have chosen for this anthology.

While reading the books in my gardening library, I noticed that the theme of scent recurs time and time again. I realized that along with the colours and shapes of flowers, much pleasure in a garden derives from scents. I therefore decided to concentrate my choice of extracts on this theme of gardening. I hope these gleanings from gems of garden literature will encourage you to look at your own garden with new eyes. Those readers without a plot may enjoy the scented endpapers of this treasury, perfumed with Gardenia, to transport them into a fragrant garden of their own.

Sheila Pickles, Tuscany, 1991

GARDENS OF REPOSE

THERE are already many and excellent books about gardening; but the love of a garden, already so deeply implanted in the English heart, is so rapidly growing that no excuse is needed for putting forth another.

I lay no claim either to literary ability, or to botanical knowledge, or even to knowing the best practical methods of cultivation; but I have lived among outdoor flowers for many years, and have not spared myself in the way of actual labour, and have come to be on closely intimate and friendly terms with a great many growing things, and have acquired certain instincts which, though not clearly defined, are of the nature of useful knowledge.

But the lesson I have thoroughly learnt, and wish to pass on to others, is to know the enduring happiness that the love of a garden gives. I rejoice when I see anyone, and especially children, inquir-

ing about flowers, and wanting gardens of their own, and carefully working in them. For the love of gardening is a seed that once sown never dies, but always grows and grows to an enduring and ever-increasing source of happiness.

If in the following chapters I have laid special stress upon gardening for beautiful effect, it is because it is the way of gardening that I love best, and understand most of, and that seems to me capable of giving the greatest amount of pleasure. I am strongly for treating garden and wooded ground in a pictorial way, mainly with large effects, and in the second place with lesser beautiful incidents, and for so arranging plants and trees and grassy spaces that they look happy and at home, and make no parade of conscious effort. I try for beauty and harmony everywhere, and especially for harmony of colour. A garden so treated gives the delightful feeling of repose, and refreshment, and purest enjoyment of beauty, that seems to my understanding to be the best fulfilment of its purpose; while to the diligent worker its happiness is like the offering of a constant hymn of praise. For I hold that the best purpose of a garden is to give delight and to give refreshment of mind, to soothe, to refine, and to lift-up the heart in a spirit of praise and thankfulness.

FROM *WOOD AND GARDEN* BY GETRUDE JEKYLL, 1843-1932

NOSE TWISTERS

I<small>N THIS</small> cold winter of 1960 – cold, that is, in the Maine coastal town from which I write – I have been thinking about the fragrance of flowers, a subject that has occupied my mind and nose all year, but one that the garden-catalogue writers, except for the rose growers, tend to neglect. Even the rose men, because they are stuck with a great many scentless varieties, do not give it the emphasis they might. My own nose is not a very good organ, because I am a heavy smoker, but nevertheless I value fragrance and find it one of the charms of a garden, whether indoors or out. The flowers I enjoy most that are in bloom indoors just now are my two big pots of freesias, a white and a yellow; their delicate scent is there for the sniffing, but it does not overwhelm the room, as soom lilies do. Colette once wrote that the ideal place for the lily is the kitchen garden, and remembers that in the garden of her childhood 'it was lord of all it surveyed by virtue of its scent and its striking appearance,' but she goes on to say that her mother would sometimes call from her chair, 'Close the garden gate a little, the lilies are making the drawing room uninhabitable!'...

Fragrance, whether strong or delicate, is a highly subjective matter, and one gardener's perfume is another gardener's stink. My tastes are catholic. I very much like the pungent late-summer flowers – the marigolds, calendulas, and chrysanthemums, even the old-fashioned single nasturtiums that have not been prettied up by the hybridizers. These ranker autumn flowers, some of whose pungency comes from the foliage, are what Louise Beebe Wilder, in her book *The Fragrant Path* (1932), calls 'nose twisters'; the very word 'nasturtium' *means* 'nose twister' in Latin. It is my habit to keep two little vases filled with small flowers on our livingroom mantelpiece all summer; by September, these are often filled with nose twisters – French marigolds, miniature Persian Carpet zinnias, calendulas, and a few short sprays from the tall heleniums, all in the tawny and gold shades of autumn. But to some people the aromatic scents of these flowers and their leaves are unbearable. In fact, one friend of mine cannot tolerate them at all and her pretty nose will wrinkle with disgust when she is in the room with them. If I know she is coming to the house in September, I hastily change my bouquets to the softer tones and sweeter scents of the late-blooming verbenas, annual phlox, and petunias.

O<small>NWARD AND</small> U<small>PWARD IN</small> G<small>ARDENS</small> BY K<small>ATHERINE</small> W<small>HITE</small>, 1892-1977

A CELEBRATION OF THE SOIL

LET us celebrate the soil. Most men toil that they may own a piece of it; they measure their success in life by their ability to buy it. It is alike the passion of the *parvenii* and the pride of the aristocrat. Broad acres are a patent of nobility; and no man but feels more of a man in the world if he have a bit of ground that he can call his own. However small it is on the surface, it is four thousand miles deep; and that is a very handsome property. And there is a great pleasure in working in the soil, apart from the ownership of it. The man who has planted a garden feels that he has done something for the good of the world. He belongs to the producers. It is a pleasure to eat of the fruit of one's toil, if it be nothing more than a head of lettuce or an ear of corn. One cultivates a lawn even with great satisfaction; for there is nothing more beautiful than grass and turf in our latitude. The tropics may have their delights; but they have not turf: and the world without turf is a dreary desert.

FROM *MY SUMMER IN A GARDEN* BY CHARLES DUDLEY WARNER, 1876

THE GREAT BLUE DELPHINIUM

THE great blue delphiniums have become very popular of recent years; every cottage has its brilliant clump, and in the stately borders of large country houses they play a highly important part. As far as names of varieties go, I am a broken reed to lean on; but though I do not know their catalogued names, there is a pleasing collection in full bloom at this moment. I ordered 'a dozen strong clumps of delphinium' in the early days of my gardening, and the order evidently fell into conscientious hands, for here is a fine range of shades, and I do not want to know what they are called or to get any more. I let a spike or two go to seed every year, and when they are ripe I go round some dry warm evening to collect the shiny black seeds. Formerly I would go with a lot of little boxes (generally nougat ones, the three-penny size), and these were duly labelled something after this fashion : – 'The pale blue next the Canterbury bells,' 'The dark purple behind the red-hot poker,' 'The bright blue next the biggest Tausendschön,' and so on. These boxes were numbered, and when the seeds were sown in separate patches they were numbered to correspond, and the seedlings were planted out cunningly to make clumps to shade. But the bees or winds made mock of me. The delphiniums come up just as they like, in shades of their own choosing, very lovely, and very various. So now they are collected indiscriminately, and strong young plants are planted out from time to time to take the place of any clumps which are showing signs of age.

FROM *THE GARDEN OF IGNORANCE* BY MRS MARION CRAN

DOWN BY THE SALLEY GARDENS

Down by the salley gardens my love and I did meet ;
She passed the salley gardens with little snow-white feet.
She bid me take love easy, as the leaves grow on the tree ;
But I, being young and foolish, with her would not agree.
In a field by the river my love and I did stand,
And on my leaning shoulder she laid her snow-white hand.
She bid me take life easy, as the grass grows on the weirs ;
But I was young and foolish, and now am full of tears.

W. B. YEATS, 1865-1939

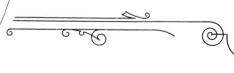

PANSIES

Pansies! Pansies! How I love you, pansies!
   Jaunty-faced, laughing-lipped and dewy-eyed with glee;
Would my song but blossom in little five-leaf stanzas
    As delicate in fancies
     As your beauty is to me!

But my eyes shall smile on you, and my hands in-fold you,
   Pet, caress, and lift you to the lips that love you so,
That, shut ever in the years that may mildew or mould you,
    My fancy shall behold you
     Fair as in the long ago.

JAMES WHITCOMB RILEY

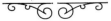

LILACS AND MAGNOLIAS

A VERY lovely group is the Lilacs, much enriched of recent years by the intro-duction of new species and many charming varieties of the common old Lilac – lovely plants, worthy of the finest days of our English summer, and none so neglected and degraded, as one may see in many London squares. Few of the forms found in France seem to thrive in our gardens from being grafted on the Privet, which often, after a year or two's poor bloom, kills the plant and begins to take care of itself – as if we had not enough of this mean bush already. How much evil Privet has done to English ideas of flowering shrubs by thrusting itself everywhere! Lilacs, being hardy for all parts of Britain, deserve our best care, and should always be grouped together in the open sun. They should always be bought from nurserymen who raise them from layers or suckers in the good old way, and should be, once grown up, always kept a little open and free by simple pruning, so that we may get bold and handsome trusses. With these, too, must be grouped such lovely things as the Snowdrop tree, the Stuartias, and bush Magnolias. The Magnolias have recently become more numerous, and it will be easy soon to have a Magnolia garden, at least in favoured places. The tree Magnolias should come among the taller flowering trees in the distant parts of our flower grove – Horse Chestnuts, Buckeyes, Tulip Trees, Laburnums, Catalpa and Yellow Wood.

FROM *THE ENGLISH FLOWER GARDEN* BY W. ROBINSON, 1895

THE GARDEN

How vainly men themselves amaze
　　To win the Palm, the Oke, or Bayes;
And their incessant Labours see
Crown'd from some single Herb or Tree.
Whose short and narrow verged Shade
Does prudently their Toyles upbraid;
While all Flow'rs and all Trees do close
To weave the Garlands of repose.

Fair Quiet, have I found thee here,
And Innocence, thy Sister dear?
Mistaken long, I sought you then
In busie Companies of Men.
Your sacred Plants, if here below,
Only among the Plants will grow;
Society is all but rude,
To this delicious Solitude.

ANDREW MARVELL, 1621-1678

I R I S E S

JUNE 19, 1955 – How sumptuous are some of the modern irises! Not all flowers, in my opinion, are the better for their so-called improvement, but there can be no question about the advance of the iris at the hands of the hybridizer. It was always a flower which depended on colour and texture for its chief beauty; even the common old Germanica, so useful in sooty town gardens, relied on its imperial purple for its popularity. No adjective, however lyrical, can exaggerate the soft magnificence of the moderns, rivalled only by the texture of Genoese velvet. We have to go back to the Italian Renaissance to produce a flower as soft, as rich, as some of those velvets one used to buy for next to nothing in Venice and Rome, years ago, when one was young and scraps of velvet went cheap. Only the pansy, amongst other flowers, shares this particular quality.

Stately in their bearing, the irises look their best on either side of a flagged path. The grey of the flat stone sets off both their colour and their contrasting height. I have never made up my mind whether the paths should be straight or curved. A straight path gives an effect of regimental parade, which suits the irises, whose leaves suggest uplifted swords. On the other hand, a serpentine writhe gives an increased perspective of the variation of the motley heads. Every man must decide for himself, according to his taste and the shape of his garden.

FROM *EVEN MORE FOR YOUR GARDEN* BY VITA SACKVILLE-WEST. 1892-1962

CARNATIONS

WHEN as a boy I entered horticulture in 1895, the carnation had fallen upon evil days. The Border Carnation was a pampered pet, grown almost exclusively for exhibition at flower shows, and not for garden decoration. The homely little pink was despised by some, and rejected by others; its only home seemed to be the rural retreat. Whilst the Perpetual-flowering Carnation was being developed more in France and America than in this country, the Souvenire de la Malmaison was the flower of fashion and, perhaps, justly so.

Happily today the carnation holds a proud position; it is regaining its popularity in the garden, whilst the pink and its hybrids boldly hold up their heads in almost every garden and public park, for it is the flower of the million. The Perpetual-flowering Carnation is one of the most popular of all cut flowers. All this development has been brought about by a better general knowledge of the plant's requirements, new and improved colours in all races of carnations, the enriching of their perfume, but, perhaps, more than all this, by the fact that it is one of the cheapest of plants to cultivate, whether in the garden or greenhouse.

If in the past the writer and other growers have helped to develop the carnation by raising new and improved varieties and races, then in turn the carnation has helped me, at any rate, to enjoy life with the peace and happiness that close contact with nature always brings.

BY MONTAGU ALLWOOD, 1926

E.A.CHADWICK

WHEN an elaborate history of modern gardening comes to be written, much should be said of the rose, which has brought to our gardens a sweetness of fragrance and beauty of colouring that were denied in a large measure to our forebears. True, there was the quaint little moss rose, the Provence or 'old cabbage', as if such perfumed petals deserved so coarse a name;

Celeste, pink as a maiden's cheek; the dainty Coupe d'Hébé, and the richly coloured damask. I love these favourites of sweet memory, and the rose lover should plead for their retention, especially those that have been named, and the following: the Moss de Meaux, the Provins, with its quaintly striped forms, Rosa Mundi, and the true York and Lancaster (both striped roses), the

double yellow Banksian – a flood of golden glory in early summer, *Rosa lucida*, Rose d'Amour – beautiful when smothered with double pink bloom and even more so in hep time, Maiden's Blush, the rose-coloured Boursault – called Morleth, the common pink China rose, Cramoisie Supérieur, the warmth-loving Fortune's Yellow, and Madame Plantier – white as a snow-drift when burdened with flowers in summer, and charming as a standard or pillar rose. I hope the day will never come when these old rose friends are cast aside for novelties which may have few of their virtues.

One of the pleasantest features of the modern garden is the free way in which the rose is planted. Vivid are the recollections of sunny hours spent in gardens in which the rose was the queen, and one never tires of a flower that in its most modern development will bloom from early summer until the Christmas bells ring out in the winter wind. This is truer of the South of England than of the Midlands and North, but at the time of writing, a few days before the great festival, a few flowers still linger. I hope to fill a bowl with rose flowers on Christmas Day, and not buds seared and hurt in the winds and rains of December, but those which will open as fresh and fair as any rose of summer or autumn. My rose friend late in the year is the tea G. Nabonnand – a poem in form and colour. It does not glow with colour in the garden, but half-open buds expand into flowers with trembling petals painted with tender shades – a mingling of softest salmon, buff and pink, and one detects the presence of this beautiful creation by a fragrance sweeter than the flower brings forth in the drowsy summer evenings.

FROM *GARDENS OF ENGLAND* BY E. T. COOK, 1908

OF DAFFODILS

APRIL 9 – The garden is full of Daffodils. Yellow flowers and green leaves form a most beautiful combination of colours when laid on by Nature's hand. Every part of the garden now, has its show of single or double Daffodils, and yet there is not one too many. Lovely always, they are loveliest perhaps when growing in the grass. There, 'the green world they live in' shows them off better than when surrounded by garden mould. Excepting one large single-flowering plant under the east wall, our finest Daffodils grow in the cool north border. One thinks of 'Enid' in her faded silk, like a blossom 'that lightly breaks a faded flower-sheath' when the Daffodils appear. Indeed, one can scarcely look on them in their beauty, without recalling the lines of some familiar quotation; mine shall only be from the children's nursery song-book –

> 'Daffy-down-dilly has come up to town
> In a yellow petticoat and a green gown.'

(Poor Daffodilla! for yellow is jealousy, and green is forsaken.) The old jingle paints well enough the Daffodil's outside. Whatever else may lie within the golden depth of her cup and about her silken petals, all the poetry of the Daffodil, has been said and sung from old, old days, up to our own time by those happy few whose thoughts shape themselves in verse.

FROM *DAYS AND HOURS IN A GARDEN* BY E. V. BOYLE, 1884

Whenever I dream of an English cottage garden, I see a little lane of Madonna lilies leading to the humble door, and many an exquisite moment of dreams-come-true has been mine when I have found the cottage and the lane! They are by no means uncommon. Our British workman has in him a beautiful love of gardens. So by millstream, by roadside, by hayfield, you will find the thatched, half-timbered cottage, and leading to its creeper-clad portal an avenue of Madonna lilies, often backed by hollyhocks, edged with lavender. And how they grow, those stately lilies with their golden throats! They seem to thrive anywhere, though I know they hate a stagnant soil. In the summer dusk, exhaling their powerful sweetness, they would make a poet of the veriest clod. In my garden they grow among a pink-flowered plant, called, I believe, rose campion. It seeds freely, has a silvery foliage with the texture of plush, and grows among the lilies with a high free-branching habit; the colour of the flower is a bright rosy magenta, which sounds ugly enough, but is in reality a brilliant foil to the satin-white of the lilies. They make great demands on patience, the prime virtue of a gardener, these Madonna lilies:

they want wonderful patience, for they establish themselves so slowly, and hate to be disturbed. They start into growth very early, and must be planted among the first of autumn bulbs. It is wise to order them in late summer, and to see that in planting they have a well-drained site, are not near fresh manure, and are set in a little sharp sand. It is recommended by some gardeners to dust the bulbs with dry flower of sulphur before planting, to help in keeping away disease.

FROM *THE GARDEN OF IGNORANCE* BY MRS MARION CRAN

HECTOR IN THE GARDEN

Nine years old! The first of any
  Seem the happiest years that come:
Yet when *I* was nine, I said
No such word! – I thought instead
That the Greeks had used as many
  In besieging Ilium.

Nine green years had scarcely brought me
  To my childhood's haunted spring:
I had life, like flowers and bees,
In betwixt the country trees,
And the sun the pleasure taught me
  Which he teacheth every thing.

If the rain fell, there was sorrow,
  Little head leant on the pane,
Little finger drawing down it
The long trailing drops upon it,
And the 'Rain, rain, come to-morrow,'
  Said for charm against the rain.

Such a charm was right Canidian,
  Though you meet it with a jeer!
If I said it long enough,
Then the rain hummed dimly off,
And the thrush with his pure Lydian
  Was left only to the ear;

And the sun and I together
  Went a-rushing out of doors!
We, our tender spirits, drew
Over hill and dale in view,
Glimmering hither, glimmering thither,
  In the footsteps of the showers.

Underneath the chestnuts dripping,
  Through the grasses wet and fair,
Straight I sought my garden-ground
With the laurel on the mound,
And the pear-tree oversweeping
  A side-shadow of green air.

ELIZABETH BARRETT-BROWNING. 1806-1861

As the green-house would have given you a beautiful flower-garden and shrubbery during the winter, making the part of the house to which it is attached the pleasantest place in the world, so, in summer, what can be imagined more beautiful than bunches of grapes hanging down, surrounded by elegant leaves, and proceeeding on each grape from the size of a pin's head to the size of a plum? How the vines are to be planted, trained and pruned; and how the several plants suited to a green-house are to be propagated, reared and managed; will be spoken of under the head of Vines, and under those of the several plants and flowers; but I cannot conclude this Chapter without observing, that it is the *moral* effects naturally attending a green-house, that I set the most value upon. I will not, with Lord Bacon, praise pursuits like these, because 'God Almighty first planted a garden;' nor with Cowley, because 'a Garden is like Heaven;' nor with Addison, because a 'Garden was the habitation of our first parents before their fall;' all which is rather far-fetched, and puts one in mind of the dispute between the gardeners and the tailors, as to the

antiquity of their respective callings; the former contending that the planting of the garden took place before the sewing of the fig-leaves together; and the latter contending, that there was no gardening at all till Adam was expelled, and compelled to work; but, that the sewing was a real and bona fide act of tailoring. This, to be sure, is vulgar and grovelling work; but, who can blame such persons when they have Lord Bacon to furnish them with a precedent?

There must be amusements in every family.

Children observe and follow their parents in almost every thing. How much better, during a long and dreary winter, for daughters, and even sons, to assist, or attend, their mother, in a green-house, than to be seated with her at cards, or, in the blubberings over a stupid novel, or at any other amusement that can possibly be conceived! How much more innocent, more pleasant, more free from temptation to evil, this amusement, than any other!

FROM *THE ENGLISH GARDENER* BY WILLIAM COBBETT, 1829

Though it is an exaggeration to say that there are no flowers in Italian gardens, yet to enjoy and appreciate the Italian garden-craft one must always bear in mind that it is independent of floriculture.

The Italian garden does not exist for flowers; its flowers exist for it: they are a late and infrequent adjunct to its beauties, a parenthetical grace counting only as one more touch in the general effect of enchantment. This is no doubt partly explained by the difficulty of cultivating any but spring flowers in so hot and dry a climate, and the result has been a wonderful development of the more permanent effects to be obtained from the three other factors in garden-composition — marble, water and perennial verdure — and the achievement, by their skillful blending, of a charm independent of the seasons.

It is hard to explain to the modern garden-lover, whose whole conception of the charm of gardens is formed of successive pictures of flower-loveliness, how this effect of enchantment can be produced by anything so dull and monotonous as a mere combination of clipped green and stone work.

The traveler returning from Italy, with his eyes and imagination full of the ineffable Italian garden-magic, knows vaguely that the enchantment exists; that he has been under its spell, and that it is more potent, more enduring, more intoxicating to every sense than the most elaborate and glowing effects of modern horticulture; but he may not have found the key to the mystery. Is it because the sky is bluer, because the vegetation is more luxuriant? Our midsummer skies are almost as deep, our foliage is as rich, and perhaps more varied; there are, indeed, not a few resemblances between the North American summer climate and that of Italy in spring and autumn.

Some of those who have fallen under the spell are inclined to ascribe the Italian garden-magic to the effect of time; but, wonder-working as this undoubtedly is, it leaves many beauties un-

accounted for. To seek the answer one must go deeper : the garden must be studied in relation to the house, and both in relation to the landscape. The garden of the Middle Ages, the garden one sees in old missal illuminations and in early woodcuts, was a mere patch of ground within the castle precincts, where 'simples' were grown around a central well-head and fruit was espaliered against the walls. But in the rapid flowering of Italian civilization the castle walls were soon thrown down, and the garden expanded, taking in the fish pond, the bowling green, the rose arbor and the clipped walk. The Italian country house, especially in the center of the south of Italy, was almost always built on a hillside, and one day the architect looked forth from the terrace of his villa, and saw that, in his survey of the garden, the enclosing landscape was naturally included : the two formed a part of the same composition.

EDITH WHARTON, 1862-1937

A FRAGRANT BORDER

ALL along the vinery border has been a long row of Stocks, Asters, and Mignonette, and the scent has been delicious, especially towards evening, or after a warm shower of rain. In hot weather the garden is almost too hot when the sun is full upon it, and I have always taken care to grow the night-scented Stock and other flowers of the kind, so that the garden, as evening comes on, may be as sweet as can be; but this year these annuals, with several others, have done no good. On the other hand, the large tall Œnothera opens hundreds of yellow stars each night; and, better still, the beautiful Œnothera taraxacifolia, on the herbaceous borders, unfolds a number of its large white blossoms, which gleam out among the rich green foliage close upon the ground. Next year I think I will have an entire bed of this white Œnotherea; it will be worth the space.

The Dahlias have been good with me this year, but I have done badly in Hollyhocks. The Tobacco-plants, which I generally grow, and which were last year so handsome, have also failed me; and so have the Ice-Plants, the Egg-Plants, and the Amaranthus salicifolius, nor do I see any sufficient reason for it.

The Tuberose, the flower which, even in the perfect garden of the 'Sensitive Plant,' was said to be

'The sweetest flower for scent that grows,'

has been very sweet with us. But we dare not leave it in our garden; we bring the pots, with their tall green wands tipped with delicious tufts of bloom, into the centre hall, and the warm perfume rises up the staircase, and floats along the open gallery above.

FROM *A YEAR IN A LANCASHIRE GARDEN* BY HENRY A. BRIGHT, 1891

WEEDS

SEPTEMBER 4 – 'The rain it raineth every day.' It finds its way through the old timbers of my first vinery, and the Grapes have to be cut out by dozens. It drenches the Pelargoniums and Verbenas, till their blossoms are half washed away. It soaks the petals of the great Lilies, and turns them into a sickly brown. The slugs, I suppose, like it, for they crawl out from the thick Box hedges and do all the harm they can. Weeds, too, of every kind flourish luxuriantly, and we find it no easy work to keep ahead of them. The author of *My Summer in a Garden* – the most humorous little book about gardening ever written – never had such trouble with 'pusley' (what is 'pusley'?) as I have with Groundsel. I have enough to feed all the canary birds in the parish. Then, besides the more ordinary and vulgar weeds, I have two varieties of Willow-herb, which have seeded themselves all over the borders, and are for ever appearing where I had fondly imagined they had been utterly uprooted. A yellow Oxalis, too, has turned into a nuisance, and spreads where it was never wanted.

FROM *A YEAR IN A LANCASHIRE GARDEN* BY HENRY A. BRIGHT, 1891

A garden is a sea of flowers   Childe Hassam

WOODY WINDERS

CLIMBING shrubs, when properly used, are great helps in a mixed garden, and I often wonder that they are not more used, but they really are very seldom seen, except when trained to walls. But, in speaking of climbing plants, I do not mean such as are trained and nailed to walls, but such as are allowed to climb more or less by their own unassisted powers over arches, poles, or some other support; and I mean to speak of hardy perennial climbers only, and so exclude annual and tender plants, though there are many such that are very beautiful and useful.

First and chief among such climbers comes the clematis. The name originally meant merely a branch of a vine, but afterwards was extended as a name for almost all climbing plants. Pliny included several such under the name; Gerard says that clematis is 'a certain genericke name to all woody winding plants, having certaine affinitie because of the spreading branching and semblance of the vine'; and Parkinson has a chapter headed, 'Clematis, Clamberers or Creepers,' and the chap-ter begins with the periwinkle and ends with the passion-flower. Of the true clematis we have one beautiful representative in the travellers' joy (*C. vitalba*), 'decking and adorning waies and hedges, where people travel, and thereupon I have named it traveller's joy,' says Gerard; and his name has clung to it, though it has not supplanted the older name of 'ladies' bower,' or 'virgin's bower,' the last name having been given to it in honour of Queen Elizabeth, though it has been claimed as one of the flowers dedicated to the Virgin Mary, and so the flower of August 15, the festival of the Assumption:

> 'When Mary left us here below
> The Virgin's bower begins to blow.'

In the late autumn it changes its name to 'old man's beard,' from the beautiful silky heads of seed which often cover the banks and hedges for many yards in length with wonderful grace and beauty....

FROM *IN A GLOUCESTERSHIRE GARDEN* BY HENRY N. ELLACOMBE, 1895

FLOWERY GRASS BANKS

Nature offers, to the tired wanderer across summer meadows or forest glades, no more luxurious couch than that of a grassy bank bestrewn with flowers. If there are moments in life during which mere existence is a pleasure, they are surely those when the holiday-maker seeking rest and relaxation of mind and body, after long-continued and laborious work, finds himself in the country, and absolutely free from any obligation of work – free to indulge in the luxury of doing nothing. How delicious at noontide to stretch one's 'listless length' upon the grassy face of an open meadow, and look up into the far heights of the sky at the masses of fleecy white cloud which may be floating under the eye of the sun, descrying the tiny black specks, which reveal the position of the delicious songsters, whose fresh, cheerful notes are being rained down upon the earth: how delightful to recline upon the flowery margin of a brook, and, whilst one's cheeks are softly fanned by the gentle air set in motion by the rapid course of the current, to watch the little eddies of the stream where the water weeds are gracefully swaying to and fro: how delightful, too, whilst half reclining upon sweet fresh grass, to lean upon one's elbow and look upon the floral wealth immediately contiguous – upon the golden Buttercups, the Daisy stars, and the delicate blush of the Cuckoo Flower – to breathe the pure breath of the green blades, and to listen to the mellow voice of the cuckoo!

FROM *My Garden Wild* by Francis George Heath, 1881

A PASSION FOR HOLLYHOCKS

ONE of the prides of our garden is the summer show of hollyhocks down both sides of a grass path; tall stems of them grow sloping towards the south, lit up in their season from base to tip with multi-coloured silken blooms. I love the single hollyhocks, and grow them from seed, which is the reason, I am told, that they flourish so well here, and do not succumb to that disease which almost killed the cult of hollyhocks some years ago, when they were a vigorous fancy. I do not remember it, but hear tales of the passionate pursuit of new varieties and the tremendous rage for hollyhocks, mostly the double ones, which prevailed long ago in the fashionable world of gardeners; a vogue as violent as the tulip boom, or the passion for pansies. Inbreeding and grafting were the downfall of double hollyhocks into the slough of disease; proof again that nature must be comrade, and never enslaved . . . she is murderously resentful of coercion. The greatest lover in the world she is giving all of herself to those who woo her; but to the taskmaster, or the forgetful, revenge incarnate.

Fortunately for myself, I prefer the wide silken saucers of the natural single hollyhocks, caring little for the tight, hard rosettes of the double ones; so I stumbled into my mother Nature's pleasure at once, and she gives me royally year after year banners of purple and cream, yellow and rose, flame and crimson.

FROM *THE GARDEN OF EXPERIENCE* BY MRS MARION CRAN

SWEET WILLIAM AND SCENTED STOCKS

THIS morning early when my garden, silvered with dew, lay agleam in that spirit light which precedes not exactly dawn, but the fuller radiance which we usually call dawn, I was standing on the South path by the old-fashioned flower bed when I became aware of the scent of Cloves. The damp morning air was drenched with it. I wondered for a moment what plant it could be. I knew I had no Carnation there and then I caught sight of three Brompton Stocks in full bloom. The last six inches of their rather bare branches were laden with fragrant blossoms. It occurred to me how rarely Nature makes or uses anything for one purpose only. Look at the Rosaceæ: on the one hand Roses, on the other Apples, Cherries, etc. Here again the Cruciferæ: on the one hand Cabbages, Turnips, etc., on the other Wallflowers, Stocks, Erysimum and so on. Now I wonder if nature made flowers for us to enjoy or for grubs to eat. She is a strange old lady, full of quirks and crochets, but marvellously wise, always doing the unexpected thing, which when done, appeals so to common sense that we wonder why we did not think of and expect it.

For some reason or other I had forgotten my old-fashioned bed by the South walk with its Sweet Williams and Pinks, Wallflowers and Stocks. Our Stocks, like many other families, have both annual and perennial branches. The annual is by far the commonest and best for show cultivation because of their compact habit of growth. But if you have an odd corner or a semi-background and desire a sweet savour in that vicinity, put in a few plants of Brompton Stock, it will repay you, for like its cousin the Evening Scented Stock, its clinging sweetness will far more than compensate for the somewhat leafless stems.

FROM *MY GARDEN DREAMS* BY ERNEST FEWSTER, 1926

BITTER SWEET BOX

THE scent of Box has been aptly worded by Gabriel d'Annunzio, in his *Virgin of the Rocks*, in his description of a neglected garden. He calls it a 'bitter sweet odor,' and he notes its influence in making his wanderers in this garden 'reconstruct some memory of their far-off childhood.'

The old Jesuit poet Rapin writing in the seventeenth century tells a fanciful tale:

'Gardens of old, nor Art, nor Rules obey'd,
But unadorn'd, or wild Neglect betray'd;'

that Flora's hair hung undressed, neglected 'in artless tresses,' until in pity another nymph 'around her head wreath'd a Boxen Bough' from the fields; which so improved her beauty that trim edgings were placed ever after – 'where flowers disordered at random grew.'

He then describes the various figures of Box, the way to plant it, its disadvantages, and the associate flowers that should be set with it, all in stilted verse.

Queen Anne was a royal enemy of Box. By her order many of the famous Box hedges at Hampton Court were destroyed; by her example, many old Box-edged gardens throughout England were rooted up. There are manifold objections raised to Box besides the dislike of its distinctive odor: heavy edgings and hedges of Box 'take away the heart of the ground' and flowers pine within Box-edged borders; the roots of Box on the inside of the flower knot or bed, therefore have to be cut and pulled out in order to leave the earth free for flower roots. It is also alleged that Box harbors slugs – and I fear it does.

FROM *OLD-TIME GARDENS* BY ALICE MORSE EARLE, 1901

GARDEN AGRANDISSEMENT

A GARDEN! To grow one's own vegetables, to nurse one's own flowers, to rear one's own chickens, to milk one's own cows, and to keep one's own carriage! – this is to be personally acquainted with the universe.

All this, you may say, is to take gardens a little portentously. It is to treat of gardens with somewhat of a cosmic seriousness. Well, anyone who has a garden knows that unless you take it seriously, there is no garden.

A garden is a thing of leisurely aristocratic old roots and carefully escorted flowers. It brooks no forgetfulness, and will not flourish on perfunctory attentions. It has no blossoms for an absentee lover. Nothing in the world needs so much love, but nothing gives you so much pure love in return. A man really in love with a garden is perhaps safer from the usual human temptations than any other. What, indeed, is there outside his garden to compare for him with the joy and fascination he finds within? What mortal honours can weigh with him against his pride in his distinguished chrysanthemums? And woman has no seductions for the man who cannot take his eyes from his magnolias. And as for riches, no mere money in the bank can bring one-half such a sense of aggrandisement as that with which you walk a friend round your garden to show him your rhododendrons in particularly prosperous flower.

Then the mere names of certain flowers and fruits give their happy owner a sense of romantic wealth and distinction in their very mention. 'I must show you our old tulip-tree,' you say, just as the possessor of a gallery leads you off to see the portrait of one of his ancestors painted by Van Dyck or Gainsborough.

Mulberry-trees carry with them, too, a certain distinction; and think what a romantic suggestiveness there is the words 'quince' and 'medlar'! Will you ever forget your thrill of happy pride when, soon after you had come into your garden, and were as yet only half aware of its hidden wealth of sleeping seed and dreaming bulb, a friend better read in the green book of nature cried out, 'Why, this is a medlar!' A medlar-tree – think of it! It is like having the Order of the Garter in one's family.

FROM *ENCHANTMENT OF GARDENS* BY MARY WILSON, 1924

NIGHT-SCENTED FLOWERS

To NEARLY all persons, however employed, the coming of evening brings leisure, an hour or two at least that may be freely spent. To the flower-lover this is the time above all others to enjoy the garden. The day is full of activities and distracting contacts and, though some of these may center in the garden, their very nature fills the mind to the exclusion of much that is delightful. But when the gentle dusk creeps in and wisps of cool air come out of the shadows, tasks are laid aside and the mind is left open to impressions – and the nose as well.

Nothing so adds to the enchantment of the evening garden as fragrance. To follow the dim paths catching little secret scents like shy confidences as we go, or to sit beside the pool receiving the message of Honeysuckle or Stock are perhaps not exciting pleasures, as pleasures are counted today, but they are happy ones and tranquilizing. The busy man or woman, tired at night and with frayed nerves, will find in the peace and sweetness of a garden relaxation and refreshment un-

dreamed by those who seek these assuagements in movie palaces or along the teeming roads. But to be truly potent it must be a fragrant garden. Without the fragrance the magic is not there. Colour disappears from the borders with the coming of dusk, the most splendidly wrought colour schemes are blotted out, Marigolds, the flaunting Poppy, Sunflowers, retire into the gloom and only white flowers, or those of pale colouring, stand out, silvered in the mooonlight or wraithlike in the thick darkness. They make of the garden a wholly novel place and happily most of these pale blooms have sweetness to offer as well as form.

It is a curious fact that many sweet scented flowers withhold their fragrance during the day and pour it out to the night. And it is these vespertine flowers, as someone has called them, that we chiefly enjoy at night, for there is a special poignancy in their sweetness not to be found in the simpler perfumes of the daytime hours.

FROM *THE FRAGRANT GARDEN* BY LOUISE BEEBE WILDER, 1878-1938

THE GRANDEUR OF TREES

I LIKE flowering plants, but I like trees more – for the reason, I suppose, that they are slower in coming to maturity, are longer lived, that you can become better acquainted with them, and that in the course of years memories and associations hang as thickly on their boughs as do leaves in summer or fruits in autumn. I do not wonder that great earls value their trees, and never, save in direst extremity, lift upon them the axe. Ancient descent and glory are made audible in the proud murmur of immemorial woods. There are forests in England whose leafy noises may be shaped into Agincourt and the names of the battlefields of the Roses; oaks that dropped their acorns in the year that Henry VIII held his Field of Cloth of Gold, and beeches that gave shelter to the deer when Shakespeare was a boy. There they stand, in sun and shower, the broad-armed witnesses of perished centuries; and sore must his need be who commands a woodland massacre. A great English tree, the rings of a century in its bole, is one of the noblest of natural objects; and it touches the imagination no less than the eye, for it grows out of tradition and a past order of things, and is pathetic with the suggestions of dead generations. Trees waving a colony of rooks in the wind today are older than historic lines. Trees are your best antiques.

FROM *MY OWN GARDEN* BY ALEXANDER SMITH, 1830-1867

BUTTERFLIES

Eyes aloft, over dangerous places,
The children follow the butterflies,
And, in the sweat of their upturned faces,
Slash with a net at the empty skies.

So it goes they fall amid brambles,
And sting their toes on the nettle-tops,
Till, after a thousand scratches and scrambles,
They wipe their brows and the hunting stops.

Then to quiet them comes their father
And stills the riot of pain and grief,
Saying, 'Little ones, go and gather
Out of my garden a cabbage-leaf.

'You will find on it whorls and clots of
Dull grey eggs that, properly fed,
Turn, by way of the worm, to lots of
Glorious butterflies raised from the dead ...'

Rudyard Kipling. 1865-1936

A FAIRY FLOWER

When I was little we had a garden which was to me a place of mysterious sweet scents, a paradise of forbidden fruits, a dreamland of splendid colour. After we left the house and I grew up, that garden remained big and spacious in my memory. I longed to see it again, and renew for a moment the brimming hours of childhood. There was a flower in it whose name I did not know. Father brought it home one evening in a pot and planted it amid the silent scrutiny of several pairs of curious eyes. We asked its name. He told us, but it was a grand name, difficult to pronounce, so we never laid hold of it. In due course buds came on the plant, and at last they burst into large purple flowers, which gave me so intense a joy that I would suffer a physical pang of sheer pleasure in their beauty every time my glance lit upon them. For several summers my young eyes watched that plant bear its wonderful blossoms, and in later years I would lie of nights guessing at what it could have been, and fitting it to all the nicest flower names I had ever heard. . . . Chance took me the way of that old house not so long ago. I found a wizened dwelling-place with a mean strip of ground beyond – the palace, the paradise of

dreams. In memory had been such beauty, in reality was such a shock. My fairy flower was a clematis, and I left the place marvelling at the happy simplicity of childhood.

FROM *THE GARDEN OF IGNORANCE* BY MRS MARION CRAN

THE PERFECTION OF ARTIFICE

NOTHING is more completely the child of art than a garden. Its *artificial* productions are necessarily surrounded by walls, marking out the space which they occupy as something totally distinct from the rest of the domain, and they are not seldom distinguished by the species of buildings which their culture requires. The green-houses and conservatories necessary to complete a garden on a large scale are subjects susceptible of much ornament, all of which, like the plants themselves, must be the production of art, and art in its most obvious phasis. It seems right and congruous that these objects, being themselves the offspring of art, should have all the grace of outward form and interior splendour which their parent art can give them. Their formality is to be varied and disguised, their shapes to be ornamented. A brick wall is, in itself, a disagreeable object; but its colour, when covered with green boughs, and partially seen through them, produces such a rich effect as to gratify the painter in a very high degree. Upon the various shapes and forms of shrubs, creepers, and flowers it is unnecessary to dilate; they are the most beautiful of nature's works, and to collect them and arrange them with taste is the proper and rational purpose of art. Water, even when disposed into the formal shapes of ponds, canals, and artificial fountains, although this may be considered as the greatest violence which can be perpetrated upon nature, affords effects beautiful in themselves, and congenial with the presence of ornamental architecture and artificial gardening.

FROM *LANDSCAPE GARDENING* BY SIR WALTER SCOTT. 1771-1832

THE DESERTED GARDEN

I MIND me in the days departed,
　　How often underneath the sun
With childish bounds I used to run
　　To a garden long deserted.

The beds and walks were vanished quite ;
And wheresoe 'er had struck the spade,
The greenest grasses Nature laid,
　　To sanctify her right.

I called the place my wilderness,
For no one entered there but I ;
The sheep looked in, the grass to espy,
　　And passed it ne 'ertheless.

The trees were interwoven wild,
And spread their boughs enough about
To keep both sheep and shepherd out,
　　But not a happy child.

Adventurous joy it was for me !
I crept beneath the boughs, and found
A circle smooth of mossy ground
　　Beneath a poplar tree.

Old garden rose-trees hedged it in,
Bedropt with roses waxen-white
Well satisfied with dew and light
　　And careless to be seen.

ELIZABETH BARRETT-BROWNING. 1806-1861

BLUE

BLUE is my best beloved color; I love it as the bees love it. Every blue flower is mine; and I am as pleased as with a tribute of praise to a friend to learn that scientists have proved that blue flowers represent the most highly developed lines of descent. These learned men believe that all flowers were at first yellow, being perhaps only developed stamens; then some became white, others red; while the purple and blue were the latest and highest forms. The simplest shaped flowers, open to be visited by every insect are still yellow or white, running into red or pink. Thus the Rose family have simple open symmetrical flowers; and there are no blue Roses – the flower has never risen to the blue stage. In the Pea family the simpler flowers are yellow or red; while the highly evolved members, such as Lupines, Wistaria, Everlasting Pea, are purple or blue, varying to white. Bees are among the highest forms of insect life, and the labiate flowers are adapted to their visits; these nearly all have purple or blue petals – Thyme, Sage, Mint, Marjoram, Basil, Prunella, etc.

Of course the Blue Border runs into tints of pale lilac and purple and is thereby the gainer; but I would remove from it the purple Clematis, Wistaria, and Passion-flower, all of which a friend has planted to cover the wall behind her blue flower bed. Sometimes the line between blue and purple is hard to define. Keats invented a word, *purplue*, which he used for this indeterminate color.

I would not, in my Blue Border, exclude an occasional group of flowers of other colors; I love a border of all colors far too well to do that. Here, as everywhere in my garden, should be white flowers, especially tall white flowers; white Foxgloves, white Delphinium, white Lupine, white Hollyhock, white Bell-flower, nor should I object to a few spires at one end of the bed of sulphur-yellow Lupines, or yellow Hollyhocks, or a group of Paris Daisies.

FROM *OLD-TIME GARDENS* BY ALICE MORSE EARLE, 1901

THE WATER-GARDEN

THERE are many plants that are true aquatics, and some of them are amongst the most charming flowers of the garden. All have graceful forms, and some are gems of colour. And the setting of these gems is not the dry, brown earth nor the quiet green of grass, but the translucent water, whose surface reflects the flashes of the sunlight or the deep, calm blue of the sky.

Then, too, comes the framing of the picture as seen before us – the border of broad green leaves of the Coltsfoot (*Tussilago*), or of the Butterber (*Petasites vulgaris*), or of the Winter Heliotrope (*P. fragrans*), or of the spear-like shafts of the Iris, or the Bulrush, and the arching stems of the Solomon's Seal (*Polygonatum*) – all reflected in the mirror of the surface, spangled here and there between the leafy reflections with the pure white images of the bells of the latter graceful plant, or the equally gleaming white of the triple petals of the *Trillium* (the Trinity flower); while in the background rise the tapering stems and graceful plumes of the various species of Bamboo.

Thus the material of the setting and the framework of the picture combine to render the water-garden something unique and self-contained, and altogether appropriate to the chaste beauty of the plants enshrined therein.

And what flowering plants can be more beautiful in form and hue than the Water-lily, whether it be the pure white, or the richly golden, or the gorgeous red, with their leaves floating, heart-shaped or oval, on the placid surface, and the charming flowers just rising amidst their circular grouping, and reflected petal for petal on the glassy face?

FROM *A GLOUCESTERSHIRE WILD GARDEN* BY 'THE CURATOR', 1903

OLD-TIME FAVOURITES

MIGNONETTE, heliotrope, lemon verbena, Bible leaf, lavender, marjoram, rosemary. These collected fragrances wafted to us out of the past recall to our hearts half forgotten memories, imagined scenes. Perhaps a whiff of mignonette as our little grandmother in billowy skirts passed near us as she went through the room. Perhaps we held the garden basket as she cut the tips of lavender, or the delicate sprays of lemon verbena, both to be laid between piles of linen. Or perhaps our lovely young aunt with blushing cheeks and starry eyes clasped a tight little nosegay, a tussie-mussie prim and neat with its frilly border. To us the fragrance of the heliotrope in the center was the appeal; to our aunt it was the sentiment expressed by her suitor in the language of the flowers – devotion.

In an old town along the New England coast is one of the loveliest, most restful little walled herb gardens to which I have ever been fortunate enough to be a frequent visitor. This was not planted and looked after by a paid gardener, but loved and cared for by an active little lady. On each side of the central path are rectangular beds, faithful to the tradition of ancient herb gardens. My friend first points out on one side the beds of basil, burnet, chives, but as she turns to the other side her eyes sparkle with a happy light. For this is her tussie-mussie garden, mignonette, rosemary, lemon verbena ... all the old-time favorites. Each plant is a personality, each kind of herb a fragrant memory for any visitor to the garden.

FROM *GREEN ENCHANTMENT* BY ROSETTA E. CLARKSON

SUMMER NIGHT

AT ASHEHAM we had Roger, a picnic, and I spent a night at Charleston. That is by way of company. But the important thing was the weather. The heat was such that it was intolerable to walk before tea; we sat in the garden, I indolently reading, L. not sitting but gardening. We had the best display of flowers yet seen – wall flowers in profusion, columbines, phlox, and as we went huge scarlet poppies with purple stains in them. The peonies even about to burst. There was a nest of blackbirds against the wall. Last night at Charleston I lay with my window open listening to a nightingale, which beginning in the distance came very near the garden. Fishes splashed in the pond. May in England is all they say – so teeming, amorous, and creative.

FROM *THE DIARY OF VIRGINIA WOOLF*, 1882-1941

THE BREATH OF FLOWERS

AND because the breath of flowers is far sweeter in the air (whence it comes and goes, like the warbling of music) than in the hand, therefore nothing is more fit for that delight, than to know what be the flowers and plants that do best perfume the air. Roses, damask and red, are fast flowers of their smells; so that you may walk by a whole row of them, and find nothing of their sweetness; yea, though it be in a morning's dew. Bays like wise yield no smell as they grow. Rosemary little, nor sweet marjoram. That which above all other yields the sweetest smell in the air, is the violet; specially the white double violet, which comes twice a year; about the middle of April, and about Bartholomewtide. Next to that is musk-rose. Then the strawberry-leaves dying which (yield) a most excellent cordial smell. Then the flowers of the vines; it is a little dust, like the dust of a bent, which grows upon the cluster in the first coming forth. Then sweet-briar. Then wall-flowers, which are very delightful to be set under a parlour or lower chamber window. Then pinks and gilly-flowers, specially the matted pink and clove gilliflower. Then the flowers of the lime-tree. Then the honeysuckles, so they be somewhat afar off. Of bean flowers I speak not, because they are field flowers. But those which perfume the air most delightfully, not passed by as the rest, but being trodden upon and crushed, are three: that is, burnet, wild thyme, and watermints. Therefore you are to set whole alleys of them, to have the pleasure when you walk or tread.

FROM *OF GARDENS* BY SIR FRANCIS BACON, 1561-1626

BEES AND HONEY FLOWERS

IN MY youth most of the people who dwelt in our countryside kept bees. We ourselves always had ten or twelve teeming hives, the ordinary wooden kind painted white that stood upon little wooden stools ranged beneath a row of ancient Seckel Pear trees at one side of the garden. Our bees were Italian by birth and said to be so amiable that they would not sting even an investigative child. But they did not always bear out this good character and we were fairly often stung and had the bruised leaves of Balm clapped upon the afflicted part by our Irish nursemaids who were well versed in bee-lore from experience in the Old Country.

My father loved the rich dark Buckwheat honey, which John Burroughs called the black sheep of this white flock, and always grew a field or two of Buckwheat not far from the hives. But my mother preferred the fine white Clover honey and so, being of an amiable temperament, my father also grew a field or two of White Clover. The result of course was that our honey was neither the one thing nor the other, and moreover it was usually highly flavoured with Mint, for just below the hives flowed a little brook whose banks were clothed in that pungent herb. And how the bees reveled in it!

Of course judged by all proper standards our honey was poor but it was the principal sweet known to us country-bred children, and whether spread upon paper-thin corn griddle cakes, or added to the last helping of spoonbread . . . it seemed to us food for the most epicurean Gods.

FROM *THE FRAGRANT GARDEN* BY LOUISE BEEBE WILDER, 1878-1938

IN PLACING sweet-smelling plants, some attention is due to their habits. Some are lavish of fragrance and give it spontaneously. Of these, in the shrubbery, we have Lilacs, Mock Orange, Azaleas, Sweet Briars, double Gorse, various Brooms and Thorns, Acacias and Honeysuckles. In the borders, Tulips, Hyacinths, and Daffodils, Triteleias, alpine Auriculas, Musk, double Rockets, Lupines (annual and perennial), Fraxinella, White Lily, Musk Mallow, Phloxes, Mignonette, and Sweet Peas, with several kinds of Scotch and Brier Roses. For wilder parts, common Gorse, Broom, and Hawthorn, wood Hyacinths, Cowslips, Agrimony, Meadow Sweet and Marsh Marigold. A peculiar and delightful fragrance rises from a sun-baked bank of Heather in late summer, and who does not know the sweetness of a Clover field, and of a warm breeze perfumed with Pine trees, and, better still, though perhaps less commonly known, an April night full of the sweet breath of the young Larch trees? All these are plants and trees that give off their sweetness bountifully, and even from some distance, but the fragrance of many others can only be enjoyed by touching, or at least, by closely approaching them. Of these the most important are Myrtle, Lavender, Rosemary, Balm of Gilead, Southernwood, *Escallonia mac-*

rantha, Bay, Bog Myrtle and the Fernleaved Gale (*Comptonia adiantifolia*), Juniper, Thyme, Marjoram, and other sweet herbs. A good plan would be to plant these in a wilderness, with narrow walks or spaces of turf between good groups of each, so that one would brush against the living masses of sweetness, the turf being full of Thyme and the free-smelling shrubs and trees beyond. What a delight it would be to take a blind person into such a garden!

The Gum Cistus in autumn gives off a pungent and agreeable smell though its flowers have none, and in early winter the foliage of Violets and Woodruff and the dying Strawberry leaves are sweet good-byes of the garden year. There are many of our smaller treasures, to enjoy whose sweetness we must either bend low to, or gather. *Linnaea borealis*, whose tiny twin-flowers smell like Almonds, the New Zealand Mayflower (*Epigaea repens*), *Polygala Chamaebuxus*, also Almond-scented Pyrolas, the sweet-scented Orchid (*Gymnadenia conopsea*), like white Lilac blossom, and the Butterfly Orchis, fragrant in the evening; Iris graminea, whose flowers hiding low among the grassy leaves, have exactly the smell of ripe Plums.

FROM *LEAVES FROM THE GARDEN* BY WILLIAM ROBINSON, 1838-1935

THE LAND

WHEN skies are gentle, breezes bland,
  When loam that's warm within the hand
Falls friable between the tines,
Sow hollyhocks and columbines,
The tufted pansy, and the tall
Snapdragon in the broken wall,
Not for this summer, but for next,
Since foresight is the gardener's text,
And though his eyes may never know
How lavishly his flowers blow,
Others will stand and musing say
'These were the flowers he sowed that May.'

Nor be the little space forgot
For herbs to spice the kitchen pot :
Mint, pennyroyal, bergamot,
Tarragon and melilot,
Dill for witchcraft, prisoners' rue,
Coriander, costmary,
Tansy, thyme, Sweet Cicely,
Saffron, balm and rosemary
That since the Virgin threw her cloak
Across it, – so say cottage folk –
Has changed its flowers from white to blue.
But have a care that seeds be strewn
One night beneath a waxing moon,
And pick when the moon is on the wane,
Else shall your toil be all in vain.

VITA SACKVILLE-WEST. 1892-1962

AMONGST THE CABBAGES

I HAVE a fancy to open the gate and go all round the kitchen garden quite prosaically. The other garden will seem still sweeter, after. Here, on the left, is a breadth of wonderful Lettuces, round and close like small round Cabbages with milk-white middles; and beyond, some taller and tied-up – more like salad. Near the Lettuces are tall ranks of Peas, hung all over with well-filled pods. I think I like these beautiful green Peas, growing here, as much as when served up in a dish for dinner. There seems always to be something attractive to Art of all kinds in pea pods; from the pods sculptured on the great bronze gates of the cathedral at Pisa, or the raised needlework of the sixteenth century, to the ornaments in the jewellers' shops of Paris or the portraits of Marrowfats or Telegraph Pea in the advertisement sheets of gardening papers. These last being really pictures, though not meant so. I remember once being shown a white satin spencer of Queen Elizabeth's, embroidered in butterflies and Green Pea pods half open to show the rows of peas within.

I think there is Beet-root, and a fine lot of young cabbages, beyond the Peas – in which no one can feel any particular interest; and oh! such a sweet patch of seedling Mrs. Sinkins white Pink. I wish that Pink did possess a more poetical name – Arethusa or Boule de Neige! but the thing is done, and to the end of time Mrs. Sinkins will be herself.

FROM *DAYS AND HOURS IN A GARDEN* BY E. V. BOYLE, 1884

Maud Naftel 1885.

A FOUNTAIN OF FLOWERS

May 6 – The month of May would be Heaven upon earth if only it came in August or September, when summer mostly begins! but such cold, hard weather as we have had spoils sadly our enjoyment of the blossom trees and all the pleasures of spring. There have been just one or two sweet days, when the white Cherry orchards shone softly against a sky of serenest blue, days when we did but revel in the joyous present, forgetting quite that ever it could be that 'Rough winds do shake the darling buds of May.'

If the Espaliers in the kitchen garden alongside the middle walk would but flower together all at once, that walk in May would be better than any picture gallery. But our gallery walls perversely decorate themselves only a little bit at a time. One bit, at a corner of the cross-walks, is now in full perfection. A faint delicious perfume steals out through the iron gate to the flower garden, inviting as one passes by, to turn and peep within. There are the trained leafless branches covered thick with knots of flower. They open very deliberately and there abide for a little happy while, self-conscious, round, and pink, and firm; then there comes a setting of delicate green around the flowers; and then, the apple tree in bloom is one of earth's lovliest sights. Apple-blossom must be added to my pharmacopœia of sweet smells. To inhale a cluster of Blenheim Orange gives back youth for just half a minute after. It is not merely that with the perfume, the heart goes back to remembered times, – it is a real, absolute elixir! Our young Siberian Crabtrees are like great white bouquets; and behind the pigeon-house there is a wonder of Japanese Apple (Pyrus Malus floribunda). It is like a fountain of flowers, tossing its pink flower-laden branches in every direction.

FROM *DAYS AND HOURS IN A GARDEN* BY E. V. BOYLE, 1884

THROUGH THE OPEN WINDOWS

'Through the open windows also, at almost any time of the year, pours the delicious scent of leaf and flower – of Winter Sweet, Violets, or Sweet Peas; of Stocks, or Mignonette; of Wallflowers, or Roses. Just to name a few of the plants whose scent fills the rooms, what glories are thereby called up – Honeysuckle and Jasmine, Lily of the Valley, Lilac and Narcissus, Carnation, Syringa and Heliotrope, Thyme, Bergamot, and Aloysia! These, and a hundred other fragrances mingled together in infinitely varying combinations, give sensuous joys which even the most jaded can but appreciate. For there is probably no pleasure so democratic as that which is yielded by the fragrance of flowers and leaves. The colour and form of plants require a little attention for their appreciation, but their odour overwhelms our senses whether we attend or no. The variety of perfumes yielded by plants is almost as great as their forms, for blossom of Apple and of Jonquil, leaf of Strawberry, Currant, and Sweet Gale gives each an æsthetic pleasure peculiar to itself.'

FROM *A GARDEN BY THE SEA*, ANON.

A CHARM

TAKE of English earth as much
As either hand may rightly clutch.
In taking of it breathe
Prayer for all who lie beneath.
Not the great nor well-bespoke,
But the mere uncounted folk
Of whose life and death is none
Report or lamentation.
   Lay that earth upon thy heart,
   And thy sickness shall depart!

Take of English flowers these –
Spring's full-facèd primroses,
Summer's wild wide-hearted rose,
Autumn's wall-flower of the close,
And, thy darkness to illume,
Winter's bee-thronged ivy-bloom.
Seek and serve them where they bide
From Candlemas to Christmas-tide,
   For these simples, used aright,
   Can restore a failing sight.

RUDYARD KIPLING, 1865-1936

ONE of the pleasantest recollections of my childhood is of setting forth with my father on winter Sunday afternoons from the commodious old stone house where we dwelt, just beyond the then limits of the city of Baltimore, and making our way across the frozen fields and along a narrow lane to a small commercial greenhouse owned by an apple-cheeked old Englishman whose name was Unwin. My father had a small lean-to greenhouse off his library where he indulged his fancy for Abutilons, Fuchsias, and such like old fashioned greenhouse plants, but what brought us to Mr. Unwin's was to see and discuss his very fine collection of sweet leaved Geraniums, or to speak more exactly, Pelargoniums. It appeared that though Mr. Unwin's was a very modest establishment, this collection of fragrant leaved Geraniums was very complete and enjoyed considerable fame among plant-fanciers about the city and its environs.

My part in these visits was a silent one and would no doubt to the youth of today seem an extremely dull manner of spending an afternoon. But it was far from being so to me. I followed the two flower-lovers, the one so tall and straight, the other old and bent, up and down the narrow aisles between the benches of plants, pausing when they paused, moving slowly forward when they advanced, filled with beatitude by the warm sweet odours given off by the moist earth and the growing green things. No notice was taken of me and so, left to my own devices, I would snip as I went, a leaf here, a leaf there, until finally with my hands and pockets full of aromatic leaves I would subside on an upturned tub in a corner to sniff and compare the different scents to my

heart's content. It was a very good game indeed, as well as valuable nose training. It always seemed amazing that just leaves could have such a variety of odours. Some had the scents of Oranges and Lemons, some were spicy, others had a Rose-like fragrance, and many were vaguely familiar but tantalizingly elusive. One that specially ravished my youthful nose smelled exactly like the Pennyroyal that grew in our woods. The leaves of this kind were large and soft and the bush was lax and ungainly in habit. I know it now for *Pelargonium tomentosum*, usually called the Peppermint Geranium. But my favourite was a little slender plant with small much-cut leaves that had the sharp refreshing scent of Lemon, with something sweet behind it. It had the charm of lemon drops – acid and sweet – and always made my mouth water ecstatically.

FROM *THE FRAGRANT GARDEN* BY LOUISE BEEBE WILDER, 1878-1938

THE PUREST OF HUMAN PLEASURES

'GOD Almightie first planted a Garden', says Lord Bacon. 'And indeed it is the Purest of Humane Pleasures, it is the Greatest Refreshment to the Spirits of Man'. Never were truer words spoken.

So deeply is the gardener's instinct implanted in my soul, I really love the tools with which I work – the iron fork, the spade, the hoe, the rake, the trowel, and the watering-pot are pleasant objects in my eyes. The ingenuity of modern times has invented many variations of these primitive instruments of toil, and many of them are most useful and helpful, as, for instance, a short, five-pronged hand-fork, a delightful tool to use in breaking up the earth about the roots of weeds. Some of the weeds are so wide-spreading and tenacious, like clover and mallow, that they seem to have fastened themselves around the nether millstone, it is so difficult to disengage their hold.

Once loosened, however, by the friendly little fork, they must come up, whether they will or no.

The very act of planting a seed in the earth has in it to me something beautiful. I always do it with a joy that is largely mixed with awe. I watch my garden beds after they are sown, and think how one of God's exquisite miracles is going on beneath the dark earth out of sight. I never forget my planted seeds. Often I wake in the night and think how the rails and the dews have reached to the dry shell and softened it; how the spirit of life begins to stir within, and the individuality of the plant to assert itself; how it is thrusting two hands forth from the imprisoning husk, one, the root, to grasp the earth, to hold itself firm and absorb its food, the other stretching above to find the light, that it may drink in the breeze and sunshine and so climb to its full perfection of beauty.

FROM *AN ISLAND GARDEN* BY CELIA THAXTER, 1835-1894

A SEA-COAST GARDEN

JUNE in a garden on the North-east Coast is not at all like June in most other English gardens. Here, this lovely month, instead of bringing warm and genial weather, often gives us fogs and sea-mists; soft white clouds that gather up and roll across the lawn like smoke. The mist-wreaths sometimes hang about for days: night and morning the fog-horns sound, the garden hardly smiles, the very birds sing quietly – a mute is on the strings.

But a wind springs up, the clouds are blown away. Now dazzling sunshine bathes the whole garden in a flood of light. The copse, the cliff, the meadows, and the sea laugh joyously beneath a blue and radiant sky. All day long the bees are humming, larks are singing, and the yellow-hammers never cease their long-drawn musical sighs.

Never was there such a garden for scent and colour. The commonest flowers are dowered here with gifts and virtues hitherto unknown. The salt breath of the sea has filled the buds and flowers with its own vigour. How scarlet are the big perennial Poppies, how snowy white the clumps of Daisies, white as foam-flowers on the crest of waves. One must believe that in a sea-coast garden both scent and colour become more deep, more powerful, more vivid, and brilliant. Where else in June are winds so exquisitely sweetened with the fragrance of Pinks and Honeysuckle, and where in July are the scents of Jasmine and Madonna-Lilies so heavily and deliciously blended? Will a time ever come, I wonder, when we shall arrange the perfumes of our flowers as carefully as we sort their colours. Those who have read 'The Scented Garden,' by F. W. Burbidge, will feel as I do, that there is a great deal more in the science of scents than most of us imagine. It is not merely that flower-scents are delicious, they are a power; and some of their powers are becoming definitely known and understood. If anybody wants to study flower-scents to the best advantage, he could not do better than plant his garden by the sea.

FROM *SEA-COAST GARDENS AND GARDENING* BY F. A. BADSWELL. 1908

THE FLOWER BORDER IN JULY

Towards the end of July the large flower border begins to show its scheme. Until then, although it has been well filled with growing plants, there has been no attempt to show its whole intention. But now this is becoming apparent. The two ends . . . are of grey foliage, with, at the near end, flowers of pale blue, white and lightest yellow. The tall spikes of pale blue delphinium are over, and now there are the graceful grey-blue flowers of campanula lactiflora that stand just in front of the great larkspurs. At the back is a white everlasting pea, four years planted and now growing tall and strong. The over-blown flowers of the delphinium have been removed, but their stems have been left just the right height for supporting the growth of the white pea, which is now trained over them and comes forward to meet the pale blue-white campanula. In front of this there is a drift of rue, giving a beautiful effect of dim grey colour and softened shadow; it is crowned by its spreading corymbs of pale yellow bloom that all rise nearly to a level. Again in front is the grand glaucous foliage of sea-kale.

FROM *THE MAKING OF A GARDEN* BY GERTRUDE JEKYLL, 1843-1932

B E D D I N G - O U T

For the ordinary bedding-out of ordinary gardens I have a real contempt. It is at once gaudy and monotonous. A garden is left bare for eight months in the year, that for the four hottest months there shall be a blaze of the hottest colour. The same combinations of the same flowers appear wherever you go. Calceolarias, Verbenas, and Zonal Pelargoniums, with a border of Pyrethrum or Cerastium – and that is about all. There is no thought and no imagination. The 'bedding-stuff' is got together and planted out, and each year of planting is a repetition of the year before; and thus, as Forbes Watson says so truly, 'Gardeners are teaching us to think too little about the plants individually, and to look at them chiefly as an assemblage of beautiful colours. It is difficult in those blooming masses to separate one from another; all produce so much the same sort of impression. The consequence is, people see the flowers on our beds without caring to know anything about them, or even ask their names.' Any interest in the separate plants is impossible, and then they are, almost without exception, scentless plants, to which no association attaches, and which are cared for merely because they give a line or patch of red or yellow to the garden. 'The lust of the eye and the pride of life,' – there is little purer pleasure to be drawn from 'bedding stuff' than those words convey.

FROM *A YEAR IN A LANCASHIRE GARDEN* BY HENRY A. BRIGHT, 1891

THE HONEYED RAIN

RAIN do not hurt my flowers, but quickly spread
    Your hony drops : presse not to smell them here :
When they are ripe, their odour will ascend
And at your lodging with their thanks appear.

GEORGE HERBERT, 1593-1633

SONG OF THE LOTUS-EATERS

THERE is sweet music here that softer falls
        Than petals from blown roses on the grass,
Or night-dews on still waters between walls
Of shadowy granite, in a gleaming pass ;
Music that gentlier on the spirit lies,
Than tired eyelids upon tired eyes ;
Music that brings sweet sleep down from the blissful skies.
Here are cool mosses deep,
And thro' the moss the ivies creep,
And in the stream the long-leaved flowers weep,
And from the craggy ledge the poppy hangs in sleep.

ALFRED TENNYSON, 1809-1892

GARDEN MEMORIES

I MUST bring these Notes, such as they are, to a close, and yet I feel I have scarcely even yet described the pleasures of a garden. But my memory at least can do it justice. It recalls summer afternoons, when the lawn tennis went merrily on the lawn, by the weeping ash-tree, and summer evenings, when the house was too hot, and we sat out after dinner upon the terrace with the claret and the fruit. The air was all perfume, and the light lingered long in the east over the church steeple three miles away, and no sound but of our own voices broke the silence and the peace.

Again, there were fine bright autumn days – days when the garden was full of warm scent and warmer colour – days when the children could swing for hours in the hammock, which hangs between two large Sycamores, and have their tea-table beneath the trees, – days when the still air was only stirred by the patter of a falling chestnut, or the note of some solitary bird, or the sound of church bells far away. Beyond the grass-field, which comes nearly up to the house, was a field of wheat, and we could watch the harvesting, and follow with our eyes the loaded waggons as they passed along by the hedge-row trees.

But such recollections grow thicker as I write, and words, such as I at least can command, do them little justice. I cannot really share with my readers these pleasures of the past, though I like to fancy that they may feel some kindly sympathy, as they remember happy days in gardens dear to them as mine to me.

FROM *A YEAR IN A LANCASHIRE GARDEN* BY HENRY A. BRIGHT, 1891

PENHALIGON'S GARDENIA

T HE heady, waxy scent of Penhaligon's *Gardenia* comes from the hot gardens by the Mediterranean sea. It is a lingering evocative fragrance, reminiscent of exotic days and balmy nights.

For more information about Penhaligon's perfumes,
or a sample of Penhaligon's *Gardenia*,
please telephone London (081) 880-2050
(or from America, 011-44-81-880-2050) or write to :
PENHALIGON'S
41 Wellington Street, Covent Garden
London WC2

ACKNOWLEDGEMENTS

PICTURE ACKNOWLEDGEMENTS

Art Resource, New York :
p97 *Celia Thaxter in Her Garden* : Childe Hassam/National Museum of American Art, Washington, DC.

Bridgeman Art Library, London :
p4 *The Croquet Player* : James Jacques Tissot/Private Collection. Presented by Dr and Mrs Basil Bowman in Memory of Their Daughter Suzanne 1939-1958 ; p8 *View of a Country House and Garden* : Ernest Arthur Rowe/Christopher Wood Gallery, London ; p9 *The Lady in the Deckchair* : Peter Severin Kroyer/ Skagens Museum, Denmark ; p11 Old Guildford, Surrey : Edward Wilkins Waite/Private Collection ; p15 *The Monet Family in the Garden* : Edouard Manet/Metropolitan Museum of Art ; p19 *May Morris* : Dante Gabriel Rossetti/Christie's, London ; p23 *Roman de La Rose, Dreamer Enters the Garden*, c.1487/British Library ; p24 *The Artist's Garden at Giverny* : Claude Monet/Musée D'Orsay, Paris ; p27 *Family Group* : Albert Herter/Private Collection ; p28 *A Garden of Roses* : Ernest Albert Chadwick/Chris Beetles Gallery, London ; p29 *Lady in a Garden* : Claude Monet/Hermitage, Leningrad ; p34 *Cottage Lilies* : Edward Wilkins Waite/Private Collections ; p35 *Mother and Child Outside a Cottage* : Claude Strachan/Fine Lines Fine Art, Warwickshire ; p37 *The Young Gardener* : Edgard Wiethase/Whitford & Hughes, London ; p38 *Young Lady in a Conservatory* : Jane Maria Bowlett/Roy Miles Gallery, London ; p39 *Amaryllis* : Beatrice Parsons/Christopher Wood Gallery, London ; p42 *Entrance to a House* : Henri Martin/ Musée des Beaux Arts, Nantes ; p51 *The Painter in His Garden* : Karl Spitzweg/Sammlung Oskar Reinhart, Winterthur ; p55 *Lady in White* : Frans Smeers/Whitford & Hughes, London ; p56 *The Artist's Garden* : Charles Oppenheimer/Oldham Art Gallery,
Lancs. ; p58 *Carle's Garden* : Renee Legrand/Bonham's, London ; p64 *Asleep Among the Foxgloves* : Sidney Shelton/Waterhouse & Dodd, London ; p65 *The Little Gardener* : Harold R I Swanwick/ Chris Beetles Ltd, London ; p67 *The Swans* : Joseph Marius Avy/Musée des Beaux Arts, Tourcoing ; p68 *A Woman Reading* Claude Monet/Walters Art Gallery, Baltimore ; p71 *Summer By The Sea* : Beatrice Parsons/Christopher Wood Gallery, London ; p75 *Le Dejeuner* : Claude Monet/Louvre, Paris ; p76 *The Summer Cottage* : William Harold Dudley/Wolverhampton Art Gallery, Staffs. ; p79 *Feeding the Doves* : F Sydney Duschamp/Christie's, London ; p80 *Girl and Bee Hives* : Lexden L Pocock/Private Collection ; p87 *Tending the Cabbage Patch* : Maud Naftel/ Christopher Wood Gallery, London ; p89 *The Vegetable Garden with Trees in Blossom, Spring, Pontoise* : Camille Pissaro/Musée D'Orsay, Paris ; p94 *The Veranda* : Edgard Wiethase/Whitford & Hughes, London ; p98 *Sweet Peas* : Beatrice Parsons/Christopher Wood Gallery, London ; p101 *In the Garden* : Octave Denis Victor Guillonet/Waterhouse & Dodd, London ; p103 *The Horticulturalist's Garden* : Edouard Gaetan Charles Ansaloni/ Waterhouse & Dodd, London ; p105 *Girl Under a Parasol* : P Lira/Whitford & Hughes, London ; p107 *The Tennis Party* : Sir John Lavery/Aberdeen Art Gallery & Museum ; p108 *Distracted* : Edward Frederick Brewtnall/Philip Gale Fine Art, Chepstow.

Butler Institute of American Art, Youngstown, Ohio :
p53 *Hollyhocks* : Philip Leslie Hale.

Charleston Trust, Firle, Sussex :
p77 *Charleston Garden*, 1933 : Vanessa Bell/Private Collection. By Kind Permission of Angelica Garnett.

Courtesy of Fred and Maureen Radl, Cragsmoor, New York :
p7 *Rhododendren Bower* : Charles Courtney Curran.

Fine Art Photographic Archive, London:
p2 *A Summer Garden*: Frederic Toussaint; p45 *How to make a Strawberry Barrel*: Percy Tarrant; p49 *Through the Garden Door*: George Sheridan Knowles; p49 *Still Life of Clematis*: Emile Faivre; p61 *Lady Hamilton of Merton*: David Woodlock; p70 *Still Life with Blue Flowers and Butterfly*: Anon; p73 *The Garden, Sutton Place, Surrey*: Ernest Spence; p85 *Portrait of the Artist's Wife*: Harold Harvey; p104 *Le Jardin*: Lucien Frank.

Fine Art Society, London:
p31 *Amongst the Roses*: Peter Severin Kroyer.

Freer Gallery of Art, Smithsonian Institution, Washington, DC:
p40 *Breakfast in the Loggia*: John Singer Sargent.

Harris Museum and Art Gallery, Preston:
p83 *In the Rector's Garden, Queen of Lilies*: John Atkinson Grimshaw.

Manchester City Art Galleries:
p91 *Courtyard from a Window*: Eugene-Augustin Le Sidaner.

Manoogian Collection, Michigan:
p63 *Reverie*, 1890: Robert Reid; p92 *The Nursery*: William Merrit Chase.

Mary Evans Picture Library, London:
p20 *Lilac*: Anon; p22 *Pink*: Anon; p25 *Iris*: Anon.

Museum of Fine Arts, Boston:
p47 *A Garden is a Sea of Flowers*: Ross Sterling Turner/Gift of the Estate of Nellie P Carter.

Pennsylvania Academy of the Fine Arts, Philadelphia:
p13 *The Crimson Rambler*: Philip Leslie Hale/Joseph E Temple Fund.

Private Collection, London:
p21 *The Spring Garden with Magnolia Tree, Trebah, Cornwall*: Beatrice Parsons; p32 *Warley Place, Essex*: Alfred Parsons.

Royal Academy of Arts, London:
p43 *At Torri Galli*: John Singer Sargent.

Tate Gallery, London
p5 *Miss Martineau's Garden*: James Sant; p10 *Miss Jekyll's Gardening Boots*: William Nicholson. Reproduced by kind permission of Elizabeth Banks.

William Doyle Galleries Inc., New York:
p17 *Delphiniums Blue*: Charles Courtney Curran/Private Collection.

Worcester Art Museum, Worcester, Massachusetts:
p18 *Gathering Flowers in a French Garden*: Childe Hassam/Bequest of Theodore T and Mary G Ellis.

Cover: *Amongst the Roses*: Peter Severin Kroyer/Fine Art Society, London.

TEXT ACKNOWLEDGEMENTS

The following extracts were reproduced by kind permission of the following publishers, copyright holders and agents. In some instances, the copyright holders could not be traced, despite the publisher's best endeavours.

p12 *Onward and Upward in the Garden* by Katherine S. White. Copyright © 1960, 1979 by E. B. White. Reprinted by permission of Farrar, Straus & Giroux, Inc., New York.

p26 *Carnations For Every Garden and Greenhouse* by Montagu C. Allwood, copyright © 1962 the Allwood Brothers.

p25 *Even More for Your Garden* and p84 *The Land* by Vita Sackville-West, copyright © Vita Sackville-West, reproduced by permission of Curtis Brown, Ltd, London.

p74 *Green Enchantment* by Rosetta E. Clarkson. Reprinted by permission of Macmillan Publishing Company, New York.

First published in Great Britain in 1992 by
PAVILION BOOKS LIMITED
196 Shaftesbury Avenue,
London WC2H 8JL

Selection and Introduction copyright © Sheila Pickles 1992

Designed by Bernard Higton
Picture research by Lynda Marshall

A CIP catalogue record for this book is available
from the British Library

ISBN 1-85145-860-3

Printed and bound in Hong Kong

10 9 8 7 6 5 4 3 2 1